Franklin Watts Science World

Technology

Robin McKie

Series Editor: Lionel Bender

FRANKLIN WATTS

London · Toronto · New York · Sydney

Introduction

Sciences such as physics and chemistry seek to discover the laws which govern the way things behave: a physicist wants to know what makes a magnet work; a chemist tries to understand why two chemicals react together in the way that they do. Both are trying to find out more about the world we live in.

Technology begins when engineers and scientists put scientific discoveries to a practical use: to build a safer car, for example, or to find a new way of generating power. This often takes time. When electricity was discovered in the last century it was thought of as a scientists' "toy": no-one could think of a practical use for it for some years. Similarly, the first laser was built in 1960, but it wasn't until the 1970s that lasers began to be used extensively as a tool in medicine, science and industry.

Almost everything we see about us has a technology behind it, whether it is a car or computer, or something as everyday as a ball-point pen or a tin of baked beans. The scope of technology is vast, and in this book we only have space to look at the more important areas which affect our lives.

As we shall see, the different areas of modern technology are closely linked together. The development of new technologies for space exploration, for example, led to advances in computers, and the new computer technology is being applied almost everywhere, in medicine, industry, agriculture and education. Finally, all technologies require a source of energy to make them work, but producing that energy in the first place calls for advanced technology.

The manufacture of a family car illustrates the complex technology that lies behind everyday objects. First, raw metal ores must be extracted from the Earth and then purified into the metals used in construction. Each component must be manufactured and sent to a central assembly line. Behind the scenes are designers and safety experts, specialists in fuel engineering, and computer specialists that help in the manufacture of the product. The finished car is the product of many technologies working together.

Excavating raw materials

Processing

Contents

Manufacturing technology

The finished product

A Technological World

Most advances in technology are made when there is a clear need to be met. That need might be for a more economical form of air transport, or for new drugs to combat disease. Once the goal is clear, the technology can begin to be developed to meet it.

At the beginning of the 1970s, people began to realize that the modern world depended on oil for much of its fuel and energy, and they also realized that existing oil reserves were running out. The search was on for new sources, and the combined power of many different technologies was brought to bear on the problem.

Oil is found deep below the Earth's crust, often in the most inhospitable parts of the world. Satellite surveys of the Earth's surface and sophisticated computer analysis of their results were required to locate possible sites. The North Sea looked promising, but oil rigs had never before operated in conditions where arctic winds could raise huge waves. New construction methods were used to build the rigs and computer models were used to simulate the stresses the rigs would have to withstand.

The North Sea oil platforms are now in full operation, but engineers are working on challenges for the future. Even larger sources of oil may lie beneath waters too deep for an oil rig. The answer may lie in giant undersea chambers, and the technology they will require is already being developed.

▷ The Magnus oil production platform in the North Sea is the biggest steel structure in the world. Its construction, siting and operation represent one of the most difficult feats of construction technology yet accomplished.

Technology link-up
Satellites are not only used in the exploration stage of the oil industry: the radio signals navigation satellites emit help to place the rigs in their exact position at sea. Computer technology is an aid in rig design and helps the rig to operate safely, monitoring oil flow and safety factors. But the story doesn't end at the rig: the oil must be pumped ashore and refined into petrol and other useful components before we can put it to work.

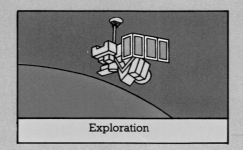
Exploration

Analysis

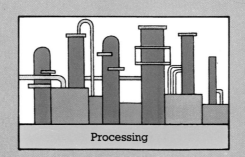
Processing

Use

Bringing the oil ashore

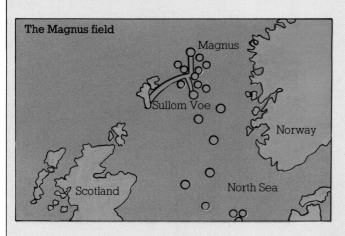

The Magnus field

Magnus

Sullom Voe

Norway

Scotland

North Sea

The Magnus Field is the most northerly one in the North Sea, and the latest to come on stream. Eight separate wells are joined to the central platform, and a 92 km (57 miles) undersea pipeline carries the oil to Sullom Voe in the Shetland Isles, Scotland. The pipeline is buried in the seabed and coated with concrete to insulate the oil from the cold seawater. At Sullom Voe the oil is stored in huge tanks before being shipped to refineries.

Oil deposits are found in certain typical rock formations. The crude oil is often mixed with fine grains of sand, floating on underground water. Deposits of natural gas are usually present too. To reach the oil, drills with hardened heads are used. When the well is "on stream," an undersea wellhead containing pumps and valves controls the flow of oil into the main pipeline, and computers monitor the rate of flow, and oil temperature and pressure.

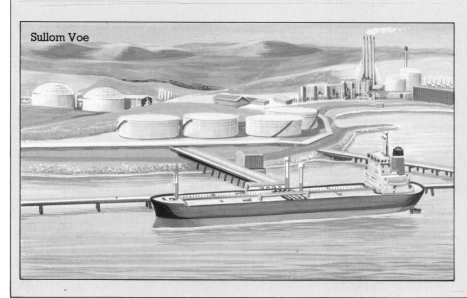

Sullom Voe

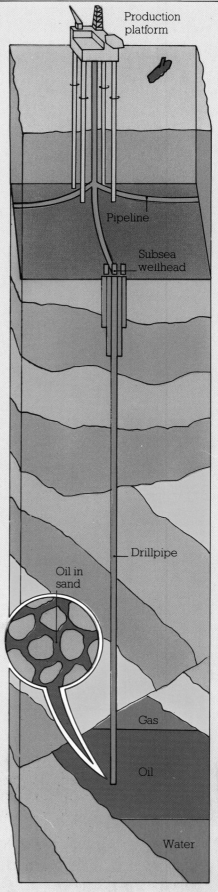

Production platform

Pipeline

Subsea wellhead

Drillpipe

Oil in sand

Gas

Oil

Water

Refining oil

Crude oil contains all kinds of different chemicals and impurities. Refining breaks the oil down into its constituent chemicals. The two main refining processes used are known as distillation and "cracking." In the distillation stage, the crude oil is boiled until about 75 per cent becomes gas. The gas is passed to tall distillation towers. As it rises up the towers, the gas cools and condenses back into a liquid. Different components in the crude oil condense at different heights and are collected on distillation trays.

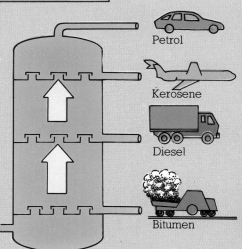

Petrol

Kerosene

Diesel

Bitumen

An oil refinery

The lightest, such as petrol and kerosene are drawn off at the top, while heavier products are taken from the bottom. Cracking is a

chemical process which breaks heavy oils down into lighter ones that are used as fuel, or for making plastics and other chemicals.

Products from oil

At the petrol pumps

Most people associate oil with energy – they think of the petrol that runs our cars, the kerosene used by aircraft, the oil that fuels home central heating systems and that which is burned to generate electricity in power stations. But crude oil is the source of a surprisingly large range of products that we use in everyday life. Many of the products of oil refineries are used by the petrochemicals industry to create different plastics, fertilizers, insecticides and even drugs. Polyester and nylon clothing, hi-fi discs, lipsticks and other cosmetics, detergents, paints

and plastics of every kind are all oil products that are found in our homes. And when we turn on the light, the electricity we use may have been generated by burning oil in power stations.

Everyday products made from oil-based materials

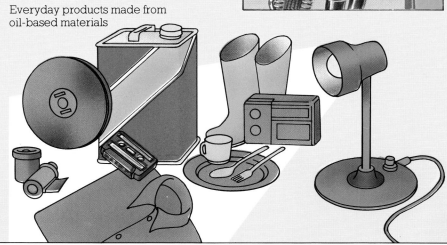

Generating Electricity

Electricity is the most convenient and versatile form of power we have. It can be sent efficiently and cheaply over long distances, and can be used for heating, lighting, and for running electrical appliances and industrial equipment.

Faced with diminishing supplies of oil, scientists and engineers have developed alternative power-generating technologies. In the 1950s, the energy released by splitting atoms – the same energy that is released destructively in an atomic bomb – was tamed to provide a heat source to generate electricity. The same amount of nuclear fuel – usually uranium – has over three million times the power potential of a fuel such as coal. But nuclear power has its drawbacks – dangerous wastes are produced and the event of a reactor failure could prove disastrous. Although the safety record of the nuclear industry is impressive, many people feel that the risks may outweigh the benefits.

Other "cleaner" technologies have been developed: hydro-electric power stations are major electricity producers in many parts of the world, and prototype power stations that harness the power of the wind, ocean tides, waves and Sun are already in operation. But the most exciting area of development lies in fusion power. This is an attempt to reproduce on Earth the reactions that power the Sun. Already, fusion power has been created under experimental conditions, but it may be at least fifty years before the technology is developed that allows operational fusion power stations to be built.

▷ Nuclear power supplies the UK with about 15 per cent of its electricity. In the US the figure is about 10 per cent, and in France nearly 40 per cent.

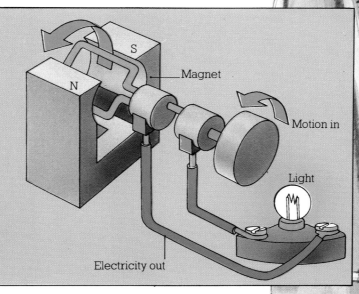

Making electricity
Electricity is generated by turning a wire coil in a magnetic field. The energy of motion used to turn the wire is converted to electrical energy – in a bicycle dynamo light, the motion is supplied by the bicycle's wheel. In most types of power stations – oil, coal or nuclear powered – the motion is created by jets of steam.

S

N

Magnet

Motion in

Light

Electricity out

Power sources

Coal, oil and gas are the fuels used by the great majority of the world's power stations. Hydro-electric power stations harness the energy in moving water. They are completely pollution-free and use a renewable resource – the water never runs out. But hydro-electric power stations can only be built where there is an adequate water supply, either from mountain rivers, or from dams.

Coal

Oil

Gas

Hydro-electric power

Generating electrical power

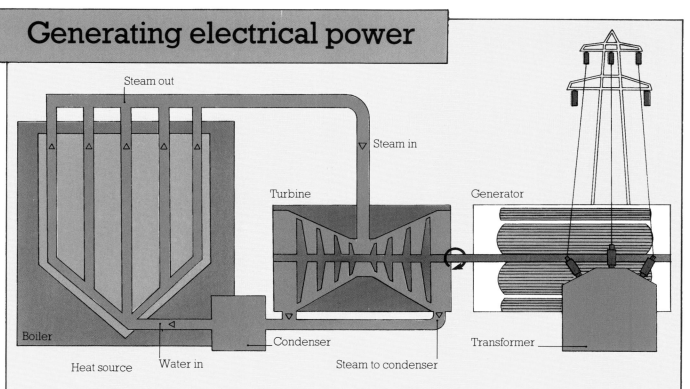

Steam out

Turbine

Generator

Boiler

Heat source

Water in

Condenser

Steam to condenser

Transformer

Steam in

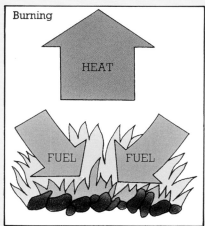

Burning

HEAT

FUEL   FUEL

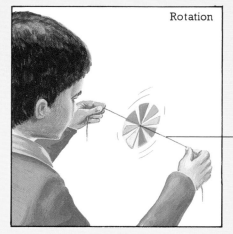

Rotation

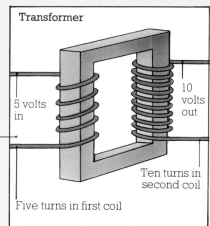

Transformer

5 volts in

10 volts out

Ten turns in second coil

Five turns in first coil

The energy of heat
In gas, oil and coal fuelled power stations, the fuel is burned to boil water. The steam produced creates the motion necessary to create electricity. In nuclear power stations the principle is exactly the same, but the heat energy comes from splitting atoms of uranium. In order to do this safely, and to contain the intense heat produced, nuclear reactors require expensive engineering technology.

The turbine and generator
Steam generated by the boiler, or in the nuclear reactor core, is passed to the turbine. Under steam pressure, the blades and shaft of the turbine rotate. The shaft passes to the generator, turning a huge electromagnet, so generating electricity in the wire coils that surround the magnet. The steam passes into a condenser, where it is cooled and the water is returned to the boiler.

The transformer
In most power stations electricity is generated at 25,000 volts. For efficient distribution, the voltage is increased in a transformer. This consists of two coils of wire wrapped around two sides of an iron core. The electric current in the first coil sets up a current in the second. If there are twice as many turns in the second coil, the voltage set up in it will be twice as much as that in the first.

Distributing power

From power stations, electricity stepped up to over 130,000 volts, or sometimes 400,000 volts, is transmitted through pylon wires or underground cables to electricity sub-stations. Here, transformers reduce the voltage to levels suitable for local distribution. Heavy industries, such as steel plants, require about 33,000 volts, while lighter industries receive a supply of 11,000 volts. The electricity we receive in our homes is reduced to 240 volts. The national or regional supply grids are controlled by engineers in central control rooms. They make sure that supply meets the changes in demand, shutting down generators when demand is low, or switching others in during peak periods.

Power lines

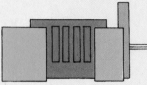
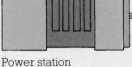

Power station

Transformer to increase voltage

Power lines

Transformer to reduce voltage

Domestic supply

Using electricity in the home

When we use electricity, we convert electrical energy into another form of energy, usually that of heat or motion. The electrical motors that power such devices as washing machines, drills or food mixers work on the same principle as generators, but in the opposite way. The motor changes the energy of electricity back into the energy of motion. Lighting and heating make up the largest part of electricity use at home. But in many homes, much of this energy is wasted, with heat escaping through poorly insulated walls and roofs.

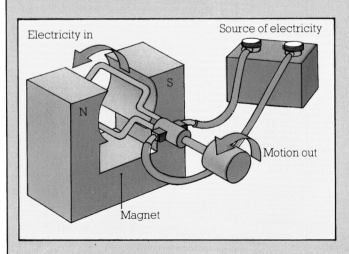
Electricity in

Source of electricity

S

N

Motion out

Magnet

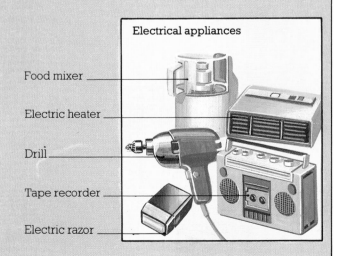
Electrical appliances

Food mixer

Electric heater

Drill

Tape recorder

Electric razor

13

The Computer Revolution

The computer revolution has been one of the most impressive success stories of modern technology. If aircraft technology had advanced in a comparable way in the last twenty-five years, a modern jetliner would now cost about £250, and would be able to circle the globe in less than half an hour on a minimal amount of fuel. That's an indication of how computers have increased in computing power and efficiency, while tumbling in cost.

The personal computer available on the market now has the computing power of the most powerful full-size machines in use in the 1960s. It has the ability to store vast amounts of information, and to compare and process figures, words, and even images.

Computers are flexible machines: their computing power can be applied in areas as diverse as education, industry, medicine and even agriculture. Already, office work has been transformed, with bulky and inefficient paper files replaced by computer storage offering almost instant access to the information they contain.

At the heart of these advances lies the silicon chip, a small sliver of material on which thousands of tiny electrical circuits can be printed, capable of performing over a million calculations per second. But the technology is improving all the time: by the 1990s, computer technologists predict that 10 *million* circuits will be squeezed onto the chip, giving us almost unimaginable computing power.

▷ The Starlink computer system links six astronomical centres in the UK Scientists can exchange information at the touch of a button.

What a computer does

A computer's job is to handle information. This is fed in through input devices such as a keyboard, and translated into the electrical code the computer uses. It passes from temporary storage to the processing unit, where the computing operations are made. The results are fed out, via the memory, to be displayed, either as words, figures or graphics, on output devices such as printers or TV screens.

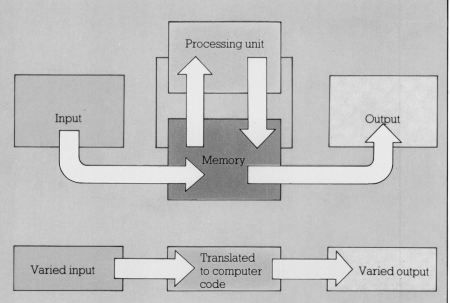

Processing unit

Input

Output

Memory

Varied input → Translated to computer code → Varied output

The microchip

The complex circuits printed on a microchip look almost like the streets of a city seen from the windows of an aircraft. Millions of pulses of electricity flow through these circuits each second while the computer is working. Each chip is sealed and mounted in a ceramic case for protection. The tiny prongs attached to it are made of gold or aluminium, and allow the chip to be connected to other circuits.

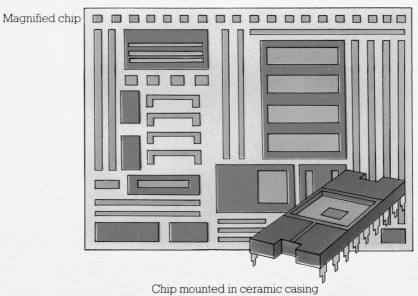

Magnified chip

Chip mounted in ceramic casing

The scale of computers

The largest computers are called mainframes. These tend to be used by large companies, or by meteorologists who need to analyse vast amounts of information very quickly. Next come minicomputers, useful in smaller offices. Lastly, there's the microcomputer – cheap enough to be placed in homes and schools.

The minicomputer with additional storage devices is a powerful machine.

The microcomputer brought computing within the reach of almost everyone.

Mainframes require large storage areas. They can be used by many people at the same time.

A complete system

All computers, no matter what their computing power, require the same elements to make up a complete computer system. The computing unit itself has a keyboard which allows information to be fed in and also has a limited storage capacity. This can be increased by add-on storage devices such as magnetic tapes and disks. Information stored in this way can be fed directly into the system. Output can be displayed on a TV screen, printed, or stored on tape or disk.

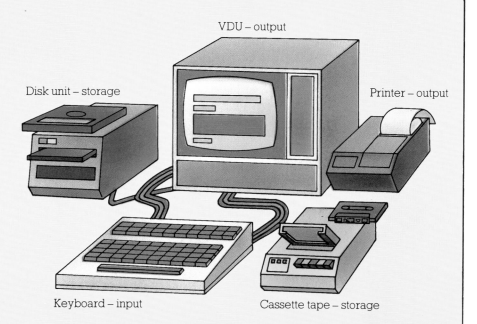

VDU – output

Disk unit – storage

Printer – output

Keyboard – input

Cassette tape – storage

Computer design

One of the most exciting areas of computer applications is in using their ability to process images. Designers and engineers can "draw" directly on to TV screens to test new ideas. A new aircraft design, for example, can be created on the screen and subjected to many of the stresses it would have during its operational life. Such computer-aided-design, as it is called, can save large amounts of money, and is now being used to create more powerful chip circuits for the future.

Technical design with a computer

Computer control

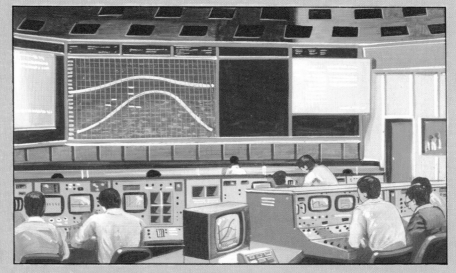
NASA mission control

Imagine that you run a factory, with thousands of components coming onto the production line each day. Or that you have to run a busy transport service – San Francisco's subway, for example, or the Metro in Paris. In such situations the computer comes into its own. Because it can deal with large amounts of information very quickly, a computer is the ideal tool to control and monitor complex systems such as these. It can check that components are arriving on the production line, or that the trains are running according to schedule. On a more impressive scale, computers are vital to space missions. The space shuttle's computers, for example, are given over 500,000 instructions that are essential to each flight. During a mission, they have to monitor the performance of thousands of the shuttle's systems. Without the speed of computer operations, such missions would be impossible.

Exploiting Space

The launch of Sputnik 1, by the Soviet Union in 1957, marked the beginning of the Space Age. Since then, thousands of satellites have been sent up, and there have been exciting manned space missions, particularly the American Apollo series which landed the first men on the Moon.

Both satellite launches and manned missions require highly advanced technology. The rockets needed to launch satellites beyond the pull of Earth's gravity must be both powerful and reliable. Extra-tough metals are needed to withstand the great strains that rockets are subjected to. Manned re-entry vehicles must be protected with materials that can withstand the temperatures of more than 1,000°C (2,100°F) that are experienced as spacecraft re-enter the Earth's atmosphere.

Space technology has brought many benefits to our everyday lives. Satellites relay radio and television programmes, international telephone calls, and help ships and aircraft in navigation. The successful development of the space shuttle has made possible new developments in satellite technology. The shuttle is a reusable spacecraft, designed to take satellites into orbit more cheaply than was possible in the past. The shuttle crews will be able to repair satellites in space, or carry them back to Earth if a major overhaul is needed.

▷ A fleet of space shuttles has been built by the United States to ferry satellites and astronauts into space. The shuttle orbits over 200 km (124 miles) above Earth.

Blast off
The shuttle is launched by its own three liquid fuel engines, plus two rocket boosters which are attached to its giant fuel tank. It can carry loads of up to 30 tonnes (29.5 tons).

In orbit
Just before the shuttle enters orbit, first the spent boosters, and then the empty fuel tank are jettisoned. In orbit, its payload is released from the cargo bay in the centre of the shuttle's fuselage.

Return to Earth
On re-entry, the shuttle fires its engines to slow down and then glides home, protected from the heat by special ceramic tiles. On landing, the shuttle is travelling at more than 320 km/h (200 mph).

Satellite communication

Achieving orbit

What keeps a satellite in orbit? Think of a shell fired from a gun. It travels in a curve. The greater its speed, the greater the curve. A satellite is "fired" so that the curve of its flight is greater than the curve of the Earth, and it remains in orbit.

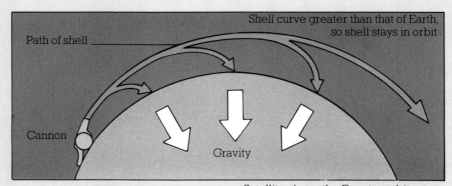

Path of shell

Shell curve greater than that of Earth, so shell stays in orbit

Cannon

Gravity

Types of orbit

Different satellites have different orbits, depending on the job they have to do. Survey satellites travel over the Poles as the Earth revolves beneath them. Communications satellites orbit at the same speed as the Earth rotates, so they are fixed over the Equator.

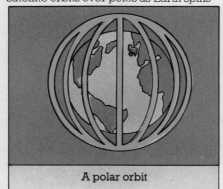

Satellite orbits over poles as Earth spins

A polar orbit

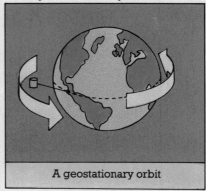

Satellite above the Equator orbits at same speed as Earth spins

A geostationary orbit

The shuttle satellite system

The shuttle has launched two of three proposed tracking and data relay satellites (TDRS). These will monitor future space missions and relay information back to Earth. All three satellites are to be placed in geostationary orbit, one above the receiving base in New Mexico, in the United States. The position of the other two enables information to be passed to and from the shuttle, or to other satellites, no matter what position they are in. The TDRS system can handle information from 26 spacecraft simultaneously. The system will replace the old system of a network of ground receiving stations.

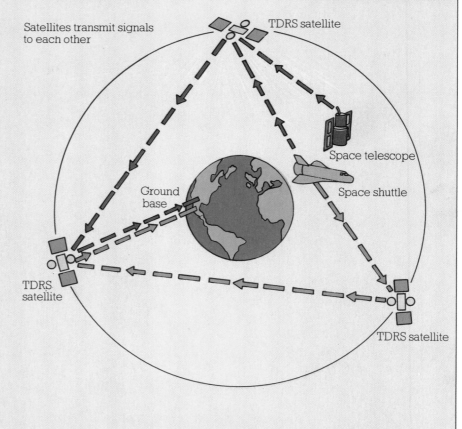

Satellites transmit signals to each other

TDRS satellite

Space telescope

Space shuttle

Ground base

TDRS satellite

TDRS satellite

Surveying from space

Landsat satellite

Computer analysis

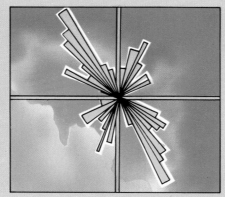

Using the information

From the early space flights, astronauts reported that they could see the Earth's surface in great detail. Now, satellites such as Landsat, specially designed to survey the Earth and its weather systems, maintain a constant watch on our planet.

These satellites are equipped with conventional and infra-red cameras which record the heat radiation coming from the Earth. Infra-red can reveal information hidden from other means of observation, such as areas of crop damage.

Computer-enhanced Lansat pictures are often used to pin-point the geological structures typically found where important minerals are deposited. Already, new sources of oil and uranium have been discovered using satellite technology.

Exploration

Satellite probes equipped with cameras and scientific instruments have been sent to Mercury, Venus and Mars, and to Jupiter and Saturn. Pioneer 10 was the first to reach Jupiter and photograph the planet's surface. Pioneer was followed by Voyagers 1 and 2 which carried more sophisticated equipment. Both went on to Saturn, using the "whiplash" effect of Jupiter's gravity. Six new moons of Saturn were discovered and volcanic activity was seen on Jupiter's moon Io, amongst a great deal of other new information.

Pioneer 10

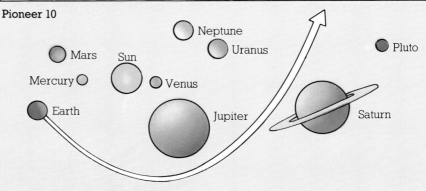

21

Manufacturing

Industry is quick to utilize the technological advances made in other areas. Manufacturers must be up to date if their products are going to be successful. And as products become more sophisticated, so do manufacturing methods. Lasers are used instead of conventional cutting and welding equipment, and new materials and manufacturing techniques are used to reduce production costs and improve products.

Most products are assembled from a large number of components – there are over 10,000 separate parts to a typical car, for example. A shortage of any one component could hold up the production line. Computers are used to monitor warehouse stores and deliveries so that possible shortages can be seen well in advance.

On assembly lines, robots are being installed at an ever-increasing rate. The first robot to go into industrial operation was in a US car plant in 1961. Today, there are over 20,000 robots in use worldwide, and by 1990 that figure is expected to reach 200,000.

Robots are simply machines working under computer control. They are ideally suited for dull, repetitive tasks, or for those jobs that might be hazardous to workers, such as handling dangerous chemicals.

▷ The latest robots are multi-purpose. This one is capable of welding, grinding, paint spraying and polishing, depending on which attachments are fitted to its arm.

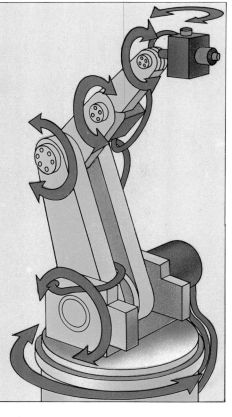

Robot movements
Most robot arms can move in only six directions: rotation at the base, up and down at the "shoulder" and at the "elbow," and "hand" movements in three directions. Compared to this, the human hand alone is capable of 40 different movements. The sequence of movements necessary for a particular task is given to the computer controlling the robot. The operator instructs the robot by guiding the arm through the sequence and the movements will be stored in the computer. Alternatively, the instructions can be fed in via the computer's keyboard.

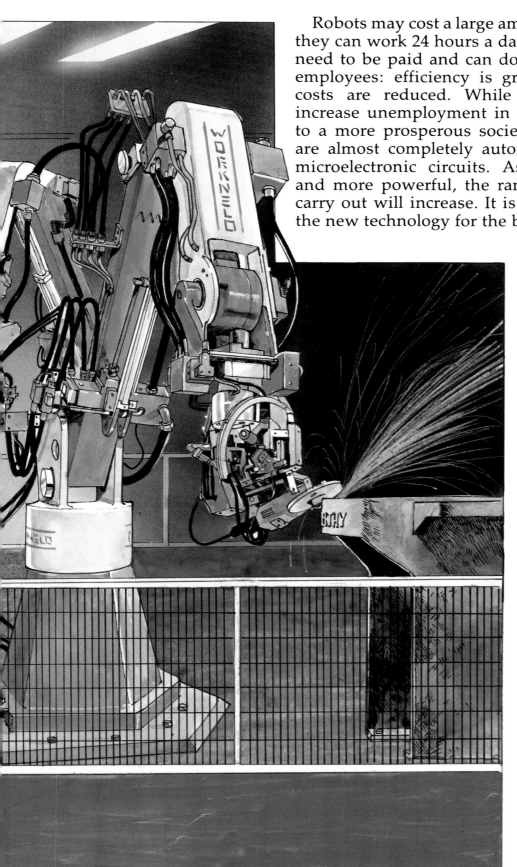

Robots may cost a large amount of money to install, but they can work 24 hours a day, never take holidays, don't need to be paid and can do the work of several human employees: efficiency is greatly increased and overall costs are reduced. While the new technology may increase unemployment in some areas, it can also lead to a more prosperous society. Already, in Japan, there are almost completely automated factories turning out microelectronic circuits. As computers become more and more powerful, the range of tasks that robots can carry out will increase. It is up to us to see that we use the new technology for the benefit of everyone.

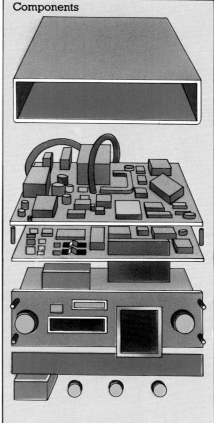

Components

Most everyday products, such as this tape recorder, are made up of many components. These are sent to a central assembly factory. Assembly line techniques are efficient and result in a cheaper product.

Manufacturing microchips

Design

The making of microchips uses highly-advanced technology. The process begins, as with any other product, with the design stage. The designer must work out each of the thousands of circuits to be put into the chip, and how to link them together in the smallest possible space.

Computers are essential to this task. Tried and tested circuits that can be used for the new chip are stored in the computer. New circuits are sketched out by hand and then fed into the computer. At the end of the design stage, which can take months, each circuit and electrical connection is stored in the computer's memory.

The circuit design is used to make a set of "photomasks," one for each layer of circuits to be found in the finished chip. The masks contain the circuit patterns for hundreds of chips, printed side-by-side. This is done using a minutely-precise photographic process which prints the circuit design on the glass photomasks.

Up to ten masks are made: one for each layer on the finished chip
Hundreds of chip masks are placed side by side

Production

Chips are made of silicon, a chemical found in sand. Crystals of pure silicon are grown and sliced into thin wafers. These are cleaned and polished and baked in a furnace. Then they are coated with a light-sensitive plastic. The photomasks are then placed on the wafers and light is shone through to etch the circuits in the plastic.

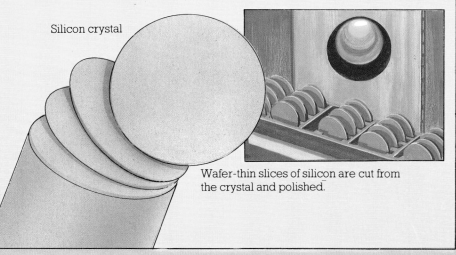

Silicon crystal

Wafer-thin slices of silicon are cut from the crystal and polished.

The baking and etching process is repeated for each circuit layer in the chip. Next, precise doses of chemical impurities are added. These guide the flow of electricity in the finished chip and enable it to perform the operation it was designed for. Aluminium connections join up the chip's complex circuits.

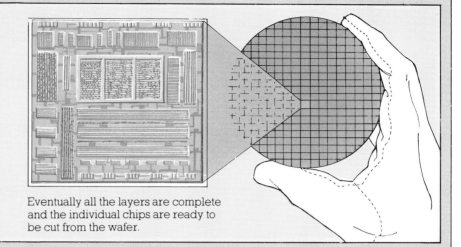

Eventually all the layers are complete and the individual chips are ready to be cut from the wafer.

Testing

Chips are made in scrupulously clean laboratories – even a single speck of dust could ruin the tiny circuits. The completed chips are tested with electrical probes, and up to 70 per cent are rejected as faulty. The individual chips are then cut from the wafer and the chips are mounted in their ceramic base.

After testing, about 70 per cent of the chips are rejected as faulty. The rest are cut from the wafer.

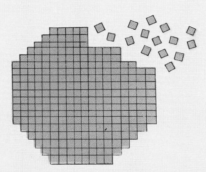

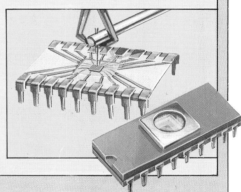

Using the chip

Some computer chips are used to store information; others perform calculations. A computer may have many chips linked together on its circuit board, depending on its size. Other chips are designed to control devices such as washing machines and video recorders. Others may be designed for satellites, or for guided missiles.

The final product is assembled: in this case a home computer.

Keyboard

Circuitboard containing chips wired together

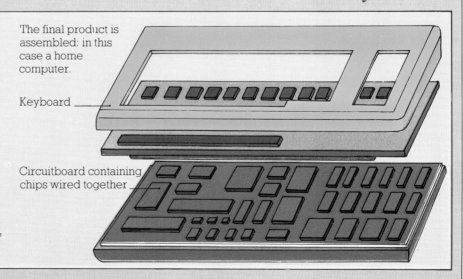

On the move

The end of transatlantic flight BA 204 from Los Angeles to London – the passengers have disembarked and the aircraft is being made ready for its next journey. Each year, more than 600 million people travel by air. Closer to home, millions more travel to and from work every day in trains, buses and private cars.

The huge volume of traffic has spurred many technological developments. Aircraft and automobiles have been designed to use less fuel. New city railway systems have been constructed, and new train and aircraft designs have dramatically cut journey times.

▷ The Boeing 747 – the jumbo jet – is the world's largest passenger aircraft, designed to cope with the increase in air travel that took place in the 1960s.

Safety considerations take priority in all forms of transport design and operation. Airliners, for example, are packed with electronic equipment to warn the crew of any faults that might occur during a flight, and there are back-up systems to ensure that failures, when they do occur, are not catastrophic. The latest models of cars are designed to give the driver and passengers the maximum amount of protection in the event of a crash.

After safety, the most important consideration is fuel economy. New engine designs, and the use of lighter metal alloys, in construction have cut fuel consumption of some automobiles and aircraft by up to 35 per cent.

The final technological goal is speed. Concorde, the world's first supersonic passenger aircraft, has halved the time it takes to fly from Europe to North America, cruising at a speed of 2,100 km/h (1,300 mph). The development costs of the Concorde project, shared between Britain and France, were enormous, and its operational costs are too great for it to be used on any but the busiest intercontinental air services. With her sleek and graceful outline, Concorde remains one of the most exciting achievements of modern transport technology.

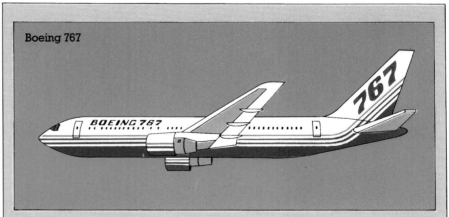

Boeing 767

Boeing 767

The 767 – the most recent model from Boeing – uses 35 per cent less fuel than other aircraft of a similar type. The increase in efficiency is the result of a combination of technological advances. Its weight has been kept to a minimum by the use of strong lightweight alloys, and its engines are of an improved design. Computers and electronic navigation aids mean that it can be operated by a crew of two. All these factors reduce operating costs and help keep ticket prices down.

Air systems

At a busy international airport during peak times, aircraft are landing and taking off at the rate of more than one a minute. It is the job of the air traffic controllers to see that this huge volume of traffic can be safely dealt with. Before they reach the airport, pilots need to know the local weather conditions and the state of air traffic congestion. This information is broadcast continuously from radio beacons. Aircraft are kept on prescribed airways – "highways" in the sky – and must be separated vertically by at least 300 m (984 ft) or

Air traffic control

horizontally by 5.5 km (3.4 miles). Their progress is monitored on banks of radar screens in the air traffic control tower, and the controllers maintain a radio

link as each plane takes off or comes into land. At the same time, aircraft already on the ground must be constantly watched, to make sure they stay clear of runways in use.

Automobile technology

By designing cars with a more streamlined shape and, by improving engine performance, car manufacturers have considerably reduced the fuel consumption of the average family car. Design of the passenger compartment and front and rear ends that crumple on impact have increased passenger safety. The latest development is to install microcomputer circuits in car engines. These can regulate the flow of fuel and give warning if oil or fuel levels are low. Some are programmed to remind the driver that the doors are not

closed, or that their seat belts are not fastened. Some can even aid in navigation, such as this experimental Honda

device which plots the driver's route through a city on a small video screen on the dashboard.

Computerized navigation aid

By sea

Few people travel by sea these days, but a great deal of cargo does. Bulk cargoes, such as metal ores, are transported in the conventional way, but many finished products are shipped in large metal containers. At ports, loading and unloading is done in a computer-planned sequence for speed and efficiency. At sea, navigation is often automatic, using computer-linked electronics, backed up with radio "fixes" from satellites.

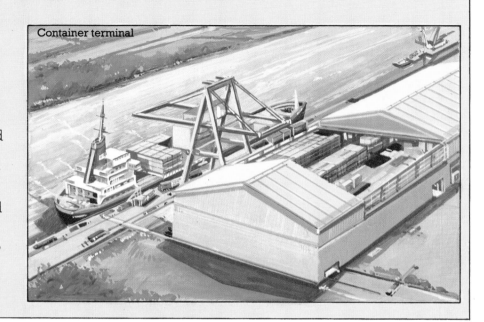
Container terminal

Railway systems

In 1981, one of France's streamlined high-speed TGV trains established a new world rail speed record of 380 km/h (236 mph). Since then, other TGVs have achieved similar speeds, halving the journey time between the cities of Paris and Lyons. The TGV runs on purpose-built straight tracks, so that it does not have to slow down for bends. But the TGV trains themselves incorporate new technology in their improved diesel engines and braking systems. Instead of using conventional signals, the driver receives all the information he needs on electronic displays in his cab. Over the next few years, France plans to extend its TGV network to other provincial cities.

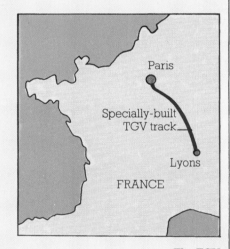
Paris

Specially-built TGV track

Lyons

FRANCE

The TGV

The Green Revolution

In the past twenty years, farming in Europe and North America has developed into a sophisticated industry. Large scale, highly-mechanized planting and harvesting techniques, the development of new high yield and disease-resistant crop strains, and the introduction of improved pesticides and fertilizers, have brought about a quadrupling of world harvests for many cereal crops. Selective breeding, and intensive rearing, have resulted in similar advances in livestock production.

Both North America and Europe produce more food than their populations need, but there are still millions of people in the poorer countries who face starvation. A long-term solution to increased food production is to bring more land under cultivation. The Jonglei canal project in the Sudan, in East Africa, is an attempt to irrigate the deserts of northern Sudan and Egypt by diverting the waters of the River Nile. About one third of the canal's total 364 km (226 miles) length has so far been excavated. Progress has been slow due to the difficulties of the remote and inhospitable terrain, but the project is expected to be completed by the end of the decade.

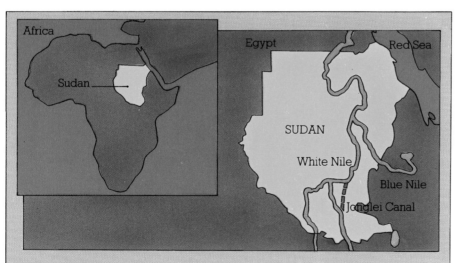

▷ The bucket-wheel excavator used on the Jonglei project is the largest in the world, dwarfing its human operators. This huge machine works twenty-four hours a day and uses as much fuel as a town with a population of 50,000 people.

The Jonglei scheme

Sudan is the largest country in Africa, but also one of the poorest, as much of it is desert. The Jonglei canal will divert the waters of the White Nile away from the swamp areas in the south, where many millions of litres of water are lost through evaporation by the Sun and seepage. As well as irrigating the arid lands to the north, the canal will provide an important transport link to southern Sudan and shrink the swamp areas.

Computers and cows

In thousands of European and North American farms, computers have become standard equipment. Dairy farmers in particular have found that their use can help reduce costs and increase yields. In some systems, farmers use a central computer which they can contact by telephone, entering details of the milk production and feed requirements of their herds. Other systems use a farm-based microcomputer. Each cow wears a "transponder" around her neck. This gives out a special radio signal which identifies the cow to the computer. At feeding and milking times, the computer

Computer-controlled feeding

records the cow's intake and milk output. As the cow leaves the milking parlour, her weight is also recorded. The computer can automatically adjust the

amount of food the cow receives according to her performance. Such a system can result in a 10 per cent milk yield increase over the course of a year.

Biotechnology and agriculture

The different characteristics of different plants are determined by groups of chemicals called genes. Recently, biologists have developed techniques to alter the structure of genes, changing the way the plant develops. Soon, they hope to combine the genes of two different plants. For instance, plants such as clover can, in effect, make their own fertilizer from the nitrogen gas in the air. If the gene controlling this ability could be put in the genes of cereal plants, then a new strain

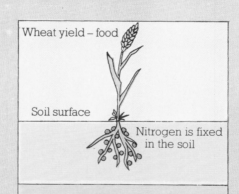
Wheat yield – food

Soil surface

Nitrogen is fixed in the soil

A combination of wheat and clover could grow in barren soils.

A biotechnology lab

would be produced that could grow in soils currently too barren to cultivate. Another new technique is

"cloning" – growing identical plants from a few cells taken from a single high-yielding specimen.

Cultivating the land

Cultivating

On a modern farm, large tractors and ploughs prepare the field for planting the wheat. The very largest machines can plough up to 100 acres in a day – a task that once took weeks. Sowing is carried out by automatic drillers which ensure seeds are evenly spread.

Cultivation

Spraying

The young crops are sprayed with chemicals to kill pests and diseases. Sprays are designed to suit particular strains of wheat, themselves produced to suit particular soils. Later, the crop is sprayed with fertilizers, and perhaps with chemicals that stop it growing too tall.

Spraying

Harvesting

When the wheat is ripe, combine harvesters cut through the fields. In the massive wheat fields that are found in the Mid-western American prairies, many harvesters work side by side. They gather up the wheat and thresh it, separating the unwanted chaff from the grain. Such intensive farming techniques greatly increase the amount of wheat harvested.

Harvesting

Medicine and Technology

In the past twenty years there have been many spectacular breakthroughs in the world of medicine. With the latest drugs, many diseases that once killed millions can now be quickly and safely treated. Advanced surgical techniques, such as organ transplants, can successfully cure others. As medical science advances, doctors learn more about how the human body works, and, gradually, more and more diseases and medical conditions can be effectively treated.

This treatment depends upon two things: the correct diagnosis of what the patient is suffering from, and secondly, a suitable means to treat the condition. Doctors now have very sophisticated tools with which to probe the body, helping them to discover diseases at an early stage, when treatment is most likely to be successful.

As in many areas of modern technology, computers are beginning to have a large impact on medical practice. The results of X-rays, and other scanning techniques using radiation and high-frequency sound waves, can be analysed by computer to give a much more detailed picture of the parts of the body being examined.

In the operating theatre, computers monitor essential information such as the patient's heartbeat, temperature and breathing rate. Surgeons can now perform precise "micro-surgery" using laser "scalpels" to weld microscopic blood vessels together. Patients can be fitted with electronic devices that control their heartbeat, or others that feed essential drugs into the bloodstream at regular intervals in controlled amounts, as required.

Almost every branch of medicine makes use of computers. They have even entered the family doctor's practice. A microcomputer can store more information about diseases and their symptoms than a doctor can remember, and so help in diagnosis. The computer can never replace the doctor, but it can save valuable time and be a powerful tool in the fight against disease.

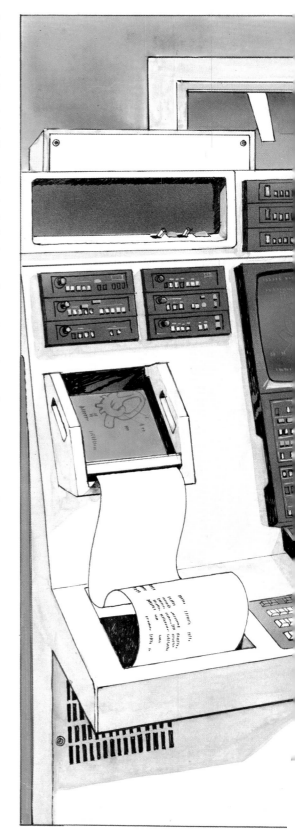

▷ Shown here is one of the latest techniques used to diagnose heart disease. A dye is injected into the blood vessels supplying the heart, and this is picked up by a special X-ray technique. In the foreground, the computer is giving a printed record of the test, while to the left of this, the results of this test are displayed on a VDU.